DISCARDED

THE ROOKIES

Doug Marx

The Rourke Corporation, Inc.
Vero Beach, Florida 32964

Copyright 1991 by The Rourke Corporation, Inc.

All rights reserved. No part of this book may be reproduced or utilized in any form or by any means, electronic or mechanical, including photocopying, recording or by any information storage and retrieval system without permission in writing from the publisher.

The Rourke Corporation, Inc.
P.O. Box 3328, Vero Beach, FL 32964

Marx, Doug.
    Rookies / by Doug Marx.
        p. cm. — (Baseball heroes)
    Includes bibliographical references (p. 47) and index.
    Summary: Looks at the achievements in the field and at the plate of the game's outstanding first-year players, including Jackie Robinson, Willie Mays, Carlton Fisk, and many others.
    ISBN 0-86593-132-1
    1. Baseball players—United States—Biography—Juvenile literature. [1. Baseball players.]
I. Title. II. Series.
GV865.A1M335   1991
796.357'092'2—dc20   91-520
[B]   CIP
                                                                                                          AC

Series Editor: Gregory Lee
Editor: Marguerite Aronowitz
Book design and production: The Creative Spark, Capistrano Beach, CA
Cover photograph: John Swart/ALLSPORT USA
Consultant: Chris Rourke

Contents

The Rookie Ballplayer	5
Pitchers	11
Catchers	15
First Basemen	19
Second Basemen	23
Third Basemen	29
Shortstops	33
Outfielders	37
Out To Break The Records	43
Glossary	46
Bibliography	47
Index	48

First baseman Mark McGwire is one of a handful of players to win every Rookie of the Year ballot.

The Rookie Ballplayer

"**H**ey, rook!" a crusty old veteran hollers to a young player from the minor leagues. "Pick up the ball bag—and, while you're at it, get the bats and towels, too."

So it goes for the "rook," or the rookie, a first-year player on a baseball team. Big league veterans, managers and coaches like to "razz," or tease rookies and give them a bad time. On the field or in the locker room, rookies are always the butt of practical jokes. No matter how good they are, rookies always have to pay some dues before they can be full-fledged members of the team. It is all in fun, of course, but a ritual that must be endured.

Yet no matter how lowly their status in the dugout or locker room, rookies are often the most exciting players to watch on the field. They arrive from high school, college or minor league play. They've come up to the "show," or major leagues, and are the game's future. Rookies are "hungry." Young, brash, full of confidence and raw talent, they are out to prove themselves. Often they do more than just prove themselves. Some of them are so good that they show their elders how the game should really be played.

In this book we will meet the great rookies who won the Rookie of the Year award and went on to outstanding careers. Their ranks include many of the greatest players of all time, men like Jackie Robinson and Willie Mays, Pete Rose and Dwight Gooden. We will

Jackie Robinson, the first black player in the majors, was also the very first national Rookie of the Year.

also meet a few rookies who, after spectacular first seasons, failed to live up to their early promise. Who, for example, remembers these Rookie of the Year winners of the '50s: Sam Jethroe, Walt Dropo, Harry Byrd and Bobby Grim?

And let's not forget the "also-rans": players who did not win the prize. Believe it or not, neither All-Star shortstop Ozzie Smith or the amazing center fielder Kirby Puckett won the Rookie of the Year award!

History

Nobody really knows where the baseball word

rookie came from. Some people think that it is slang for recruit, as in new soldier. In baseball, it is the name given to any first-year ballplayer. True, "rookie" has the ring of a put-down, but it remains a term of affection.

Although the word rookie is at least as old as the game itself, it was not until 1940 that somebody thought of giving an annual award to the best new major league player. In that year, the Chicago chapter of the Baseball Writers' Association of America (BBWAA) created the first Rookie of the Year award. Hall of Fame shortstop Lou Boudreau won the honor. The BBWAA is also the selection committee for the Most Valuable Player (MVP) award and the Hall of Fame.

In 1947, the award went national. Baseball writers from each major league city voted, and Jackie Robinson was selected as the first nationally recognized winner of the Rookie of the Year award. In 1949, the writers began choosing a player from each league. In 1987, the name of the award was changed to the Jackie Robinson Award.

Over the years there has been much technical discussion about the definition of a rookie. Today, a player is eligible for the award if he had:
- no more than 130 at-bats;
- no more than 45 innings pitched;
- or no more than 45 days on a major league roster before September 1st of a given season.

For example, a player called up from the minors in mid-September will officially be a rookie the next season (if he does not go over these limits).

Only seven players were selected as Rookies of the Year by winning every vote. They are Frank Robinson (1956), Orlando Cepeda (1958), Willie McCovey (1959), Carlton Fisk (1972), Vince Coleman (1985), Benito

In 1985 Cardinal outfielder Vince Coleman was named top rookie in the National League, where he now piles up stolen bases for the New York Mets.

Santiago (1987), and Mark McGwire (1987).

That such a small number of players won this honor "hands down" suggests how difficult the voting can be. All seven of these players proved to be true champions, but first-year statistics are not always proof of a player's future greatness. For example, in 1952 pitcher Joe Black of the Brooklyn Dodgers won the award after turning in a 15-4 won-loss record. He had a 2.15 earned run average (ERA). Black received 19 voting points out of a possible 24. Black never matched his rookie-year success, however, and retired six years later. But here are two rookies he beat out for the award: knuckleball pitcher Hoyt Wilhelm, who got three votes; and power-hitting third baseman Eddie Matthews, who received one. Who could have guessed these two rookies would one day enter the Hall of Fame!

"Newk"—Don Newcombe, the talented pitcher of the Brooklyn Dodgers, was a sensation in his first season (1949).

Pitchers

With the exception of outfielders, pitchers have won more Rookie of the Year awards than players in any other position. The first, and one of the best, was Don "Newk" Newcombe, who turned in a 17-8 won-loss record his rookie year with the Brooklyn Dodgers. One of the first black big-league pitchers, he joined the Dodgers in 1949, two years after Jackie Robinson. Newcombe's hot fastball and dizzying curve served him well throughout a ten-year career. He made many playoff and World Series appearances. In 1956 he posted his best season record, winning 27 games and losing only seven.

Perhaps the greatest Rookie of the Year pitcher is Tom Seaver, without a doubt one of the greatest right-handers in baseball history. Seaver started out with the Mets in 1967, impressing everyone with his 16-13 record and 2.76 ERA.

You might ask yourself, what is so

Fernando Valenzuela

Mets ace pitcher Tom Seaver made a great debut in 1967 with a 16-13 record and a 2.76 ERA.

great about a 16-13 won-loss record? The answer is simple. As a team, the Mets lost a lot and didn't provide much offensive support for their pitchers. Seaver was lucky enough to play nearly 20 seasons without injury. But he was also unlucky in that the teams he played for—the Mets, the Reds, the White Sox and the Red Sox—were often sub-.500 teams. The fact that he finished with a lifetime 311-205 record is nothing short of fantastic. Think of how many of those losses might have been wins if he had been playing for better teams.

During the 1980s, five pitchers won the Rookie of the Year award: Steve Howe (1980), Fernando Valenzuela (1981), Dave Righetti (1981), Dwight Gooden

(1984), and Todd Worrell (1986). In September 1980, Valenzuela joined the Dodgers and pitched 18 innings of shutout relief. In 1981, his official rookie year, he opened with five shutouts in his first seven starts, winning not only the rookie prize, but the Cy Young Award as well! Imagine what all those veteran sluggers must have felt as this 20-year old mowed them down with his famous "scroogie," or screwball.

While Valenzuela was showing his stuff in the National League, Dave Righetti was doing the same in the American—but with a less impressive record. Today, Righetti continues to prove the BBWAA voters right, having become one of the premier relief pitchers in the game. In 1986 alone he racked up 46 saves for the Yankees.

In 1984, Dwight Gooden made his debut in his new Mets uniform. He was 19 years old. A quiet pitcher with an explosive fastball, Gooden won 17 games and led the league in six categories, including fewest hits per game (6.6) and most strikeouts (276). Setting a new strikeout record for rookie pitchers, Gooden placed second in the Cy Young Award, losing to Rick Sutcliffe, who won 16 games and lost only one while pitching for the Cubs that year. Guess who won the Rookie of the Year award in 1979? Sutcliffe, in a Dodger uniform.

Sandy Alomar, Jr., became the AL Rookie of the Year in 1990.

Catchers

It took over 20 years for the first catcher to win a Rookie of the Year award. Among the catchers who were eligible but passed over were Yogi Berra, John Roseboro, Bill Freehan, Elston Howard, and Tim McCarver. Perhaps the BBWAA was just waiting for a truly spectacular player to come along. If so, their patience was rewarded in 1968, when Johnny Bench was selected.

Bench really showed the old veterans how to play the game. Apart from his consistent power hitting, he revolutionized his position. Bench was the first to use the big-pocket, hinged catcher's mitt so popular today. Also, he played catcher like an infielder, catching the ball one-handed so he could improve his release time on his throws. Instead of blocking the plate (and risking injury) when runners tried to score, he laid the tag on them like a second baseman.

With superstar Bench leading the way, four catchers have since received the award: Thurman Munson (1970), Earl Williams (1971), Carlton Fisk (1972) and, more recently, Benito Santiago (1987).

The first American League catcher to win the award was Munson, a great Yankee hero much-loved by the fans. He died tragically in a plane crash in August 1979. His first-rate, ten-year career included three Gold Glove Awards and, in 1976, a Most Valuable Player award. A seven-time All-Star, Munson hit over .300 five

Sensational catcher Benito Santiago won the National League rookie sweepstakes in 1987.

times and played the entire 1971 season with only one error. In the Yankees' 1976 World Series loss to the Cincinnati Reds, Munson hit an incredible .529. His effort was overshadowed only by the .533 hitting of—guess who—Johnny Bench.

If Bench was Munson's National League counterpart, his American League rival was Carlton Fisk. One of the most memorable moments in World Series history occurred in Game Six between the Reds and the Red Sox (1975). With the score tied 6-6 in the bottom of the 12th inning, Fisk came to the plate and belted a game-ending homer to left field. At first it looked like the ball might slice foul. Fisk took a couple of steps from the plate, waved his arms as if to steer the ball fair, then jumped for joy as the ball dropped into the bleachers just inside the foul pole.

There have been some superstar catchers during the '80s, including Bob Boone and Gary Carter. But Benny Santiago was the sensation everyone was watching. He's a steady .300-plus hitter. As a catcher, Santiago perfected the art of throwing runners out from his knees! With former Rookie of the Year speedsters such as Vince Coleman on the basepaths, Santiago continues to have his work cut out for him.

1977's rookie first baseman Eddie Murray has won the Gold Glove Award for fielding many times.

First Basemen

Both past and present, the list of Rookie of the Year first basemen has "Hall of Fame" written all over it. Nine players have received the award, including such stars as Orlando Cepeda (1958) and Willie McCovey (1959), both of whom played for the Giants.

Imagine being the Giants' manager, forced to choose between two rookie superstars! Both were power hitters, and Cepeda swung the heaviest bat in the big leagues. These two were platooned between first and outfield. Knee injuries hampered Cepeda through most of his career, although he won the MVP in 1961 with 46 home runs (HRs) and 142 runs batted in (RBIs). McCovey, whose line-drive swing from the left side of the plate put absolute fear in the hearts of opposing first and second basemen, retired in 1980 with a lifetime 521 homers. Another Giant star has taken their place at first base: Will Clark.

From the mid-'70s to the present, rookie first basemen have made solid debuts. Mike Hargrove (1974), Eddie Murray (1977), Al Davis (1984), and Mark McGwire (1987) show the depth of today's first basemen. But good as these players are, perhaps none will rival Keith Hernandez or Don Mattingly when it comes to the best-of-the-best. Interestingly, neither Hernandez nor Mattingly received Rookie of the Year votes after their first eligible seasons.

The double threat of Willie McCovey (left) and Orlando Cepeda (right) were back-to-back rookie winners for the San Francisco Giants of the early 1960s.

Defensively, Murray won the Gold Glove Award three years in a row before Mattingly arrived on the scene. A steady .300 hitter who has averaged 30 dingers and 100 ribbies during his last 14 seasons, Murray is simply one of the best.

In terms of style, stardom and a hoped-for long career, McGwire has it all. Along with such players as Rickey Henderson and Jose Canseco, McGwire is on one of the most powerful ballclubs of all time: the Oakland A's. A big, muscular first baseman, McGwire spent most

of his childhood whacking whiffle balls out of his backyard. Little leaguers should not overlook the value of this kind of practice. All major league stars, as youngsters, practiced every day. Because of the goofy curves a whiffle ball can take, learning to hit one develops good hand-eye coordination.

With only a few big-league seasons under his belt, McGwire is well on his way to living up to his rookie year success. If he enjoys a long career, he might even catch up with Hernandez and Mattingly. Or better yet, he might one day join the ranks of such Hall of Fame first basemen as Lou Gehrig, Jimmie Foxx and George Sisler.

All-Star second baseman Steve Sax.

Second Basemen

When looking at rookie second basemen, notice those who did not win the Rookie of the Year award like Bill Mazeroski, Joe Morgan, Bobby Grich, Bobby Richardson, Frank White or Ryne Sandberg. And these six players rank among the best ever at that position! Again, this proves how "iffy" the award is when it comes to predicting the future greatness of a young ballplayer.

But a few good second basemen have won the award. Hall of Famer Jackie Robinson, perhaps the most exciting player of the '50s, won the first rookie prize in 1947. Then, in 1953, Jim "Junior" Gilliam, one of the Dodgers' most durable

> ### Rookie Trivia
>
> **Q:** What Rookie of the Year broke the strikeout record for rookies in 1984?
> **A:** Dwight Gooden.
>
> **Q:** What National League pitcher in his first season won both the Rookie of the Year Award and the Cy Young Award?
> **A:** Fernando Valenzuela.
>
> **Q:** What American League outfielder in his first season won both the Rookie of the Year Award and Most Valuable Player?
> **A:** Fred Lynn.
>
> **Q:** What National League rookie pitcher was the first to win Rookie of the Year while playing for an expansion team?
> **A:** Tom Seaver.

One of the greatest hitters of all time, Pete Rose, was also named the top rookie of 1963.

infielders, took over Robinson's spot, winning Rookie of the Year as he led the league with 17 triples.

Next to Robinson, the most famous second baseman ever to win the award is Pete "Charlie Hustle" Rose, who won in 1963. Before moving to the outfield, and then to first base, Rose broke in as a scrappy second sacker. Despite his career-ending problems, Rose will always be regarded as one of the outstanding players of all time.

Rose was an All-Star at every position he played. He hit .300 or better in 14 of his last 15 seasons, winning three batting titles along the way. His major league records include collecting 200 or more hits for ten seasons. He led in hits in seven seasons and doubles in five. Together with his head-first slides and all-around dynamic play, Rose will be remembered best for his dramatic 44-game hitting streak, which tied the National League record. As if this were not enough, he broke Ty Cobb's lifetime hits record by finishing his career with 4,256—a feat some thought impossible. Along the way he played in more games (3,562) and had more at-bats (14,053) than any other player in the game's history.

Robinson and Rose ought to make any young second baseman proud of the position. Remember Rod Carew, who ranks with Cobb, Ted Williams, and a few others who are among the finest hitters in history. Breaking in with the Twins in 1967, Carew hit .297 and won Rookie of the Year. He then went on to win batting titles in 1969, '72, '73, '74, '75, '77 and '78! He finished his career with a lifetime batting average of .328. Among the great players since 1960, only third baseman Wade Boggs has a higher "lifetime" batting average than Carew. But Boggs still has to put in many more years

Hall of Famer Rod Carew won six batting titles in the 1970s after winning Rookie of the Year in the American League.

before a true comparison can be made.

    The most recent addition to the ranks of award-winning second basemen is Steve Sax, who won in 1982. In his rookie year Sax hit .282 and stole 49 bases. After nearly ten seasons, his lifetime average is around .282, and he continues to steal about 40 bases a year. These statistics show consistency and dependability. Not bad for a second-base tradition that includes Jackie Robinson and Junior Gilliam.

1988 Rookie of the Year Chris Sabo shone in his third season with the World-Series-winning Cincinnati Reds.

Third Basemen

In terms of numbers, third basemen have made a poor showing as Rookie of the Year winners. Dick Allen (1964), Bob Horner (1978), John Castino (1979), and Chris Sabo (1988) stand alone as freshman sensations. Just like second basemen, rookies in the "hot box" seem to take a couple of years to settle into their positions. Brooks Robinson of the Orioles and Mike Schmidt of the Phillies are generally considered the best third basemen of the last 50 years. But neither won Rookie of the Year.

Robinson's debut came in 1955. In his first three seasons, he played in six, 15 and 50 games, respectively, never hitting better than .239. Schmidt joined the Phillies in 1972, played in 13 games, and hit .206. In his rookie year, he played in 132 games and hit .196. However, he received not even one vote in the Rookie of the Year selection for 1973. Once again, greatness does not always reveal itself at first glance.

What's more, not even instant greatness is a guarantee of Rookie of the Year fame. In 1982, for example, Boston rookie Wade Boggs played in 104 games and hit for an incredible .349 average, with 44 "ribbies." But he placed a low third in Rookie voting, losing to Orioles' shortstop Cal Ripken, Jr., who played in 160 games, hit .264, and drove in 93 runs.

Despite an amazing .349 batting average in his first season, Wade Boggs placed third in the 1982 Rookie of the Year voting.

Feisty Dick Allen seemed like a sensation in his rookie uniform when he joined the Phillies in 1964. Playing 15 years with five ballclubs in both leagues (nine of them with Philadelphia), Allen hit the ball so hard that a hush came over the field when he came to bat. He was equally known for his straight talk, his dislike of sportswriters, and his off-the-field troubles. Allen was one of the most puzzling athletes ever to play the game.

Before being traded to the Cards in 1988, Bob Horner turned in nine solid years with the Braves. Known more for his hitting than his fielding, this tall, muscular ballplayer hit the ball at a .275 clip, averaging about 20-25 homers a season.

At first glance, Chris Sabo's first-year stats might not seem that impressive, although they were good enough to earn him Rookie of the Year (and an All-Star spot). Playing in 137 games for the Reds in 1988, Sabo finished the season with a .271 average.

But it was the 1990 World Series that really put Sabo in the limelight. In Game Three of the Reds' four-game sweep of the A's, Sabo became the sixth player to hit home runs in consecutive innings. In that same game, he also set a Series defensive record by handling ten chances without an error.

Sabo is the kind of a ballplayer who warms a fan's heart. He plays with the spirit and joy of a little leaguer. You can almost picture him as a youngster riding around on a bike with a glove swinging from the handlebars. Diving, hustling, he talks it up with lots of chatter. Will he attain the Hall of Fame status of Robinson, Schmidt, or George Brett? Who knows? But he will certainly be one of the most exciting and fun players to watch.

Cal Ripken, Jr., is one of three top shortstops of the '80s who was named a rookie of the year.

Shortstops

In 1948, Alvin Dark, playing for the old Boston Braves, became the first Rookie of the Year shortstop. Dark hit .322 that season, and had a respectable 14-year career with several National League teams.

Dark set the stage for the award-winning shortstops who would follow during the next decade: Harvey Kuenn (1953), Hall of Famer Luis Aparicio (1956), Tony Kubek (1957), and Ron Hansen (1960). All these ballplayers proved to be steady and reliable. Only Aparicio, however, became one of the greatest shortstops of the modern era. He was a sharp leadoff hitter and one of baseball's fine early base-stealers. On the defensive side, he won nine Gold Glove Awards.

Interestingly, none of the excellent shortstops of the '60s and '70s turned in Rookie of the Year seasons. This group includes Dave Concepcion, Maury Wills, Mark Belanger and Larry Bowa.

In the 1980s, this trend came to an end. The '80s might be called the "Decade of the Rookie Shortstop." Can you believe that Ozzie Smith, Garry Templeton, Alan Trammell and Barry Larkin were *not* rookie award winners! The honors went to Cal Ripken, Jr. (1982), Ozzie Guillen (1985), and Walt Weiss (1988).

Weiss is a throwback to the "good field-no hit" shortstops of the past. A wonder with a glove, there are few balls he cannot catch. Going deep to his left behind second, chasing after a pop-up down the left field line,

Walt Weiss was the third Oakland A's player in as many years to be named Rookie of the Year.

his presence gives a team defensive security.

Ripken is a space-age shortstop. Tall and rangy, he hits the ball consistently with power. Defensively, he makes up for a lack of speed and acrobatic agility by never "hot dogging." Plus, he knows how to use the artificial turf to his advantage. For example, he will often "one-hop" a long throw to first, rather than try to "muscle" it over on the fly. Well-versed in the fundamentals of his position, Ripken makes sure of every catch and throw. This self-knowledge and level-headedness has put his fielding average right at the top of the list.

As a defensive player, Ozzie Guillen might give Ozzie Smith a run for his money. In the field, Guillen has it all—range, superb reflexes, and "soft hands" that seem to have magnets in them. In the big leagues, a fielder "gives" with the ball as he catches it. He absorbs it, bringing it into his body. A player with "hard" or "frying pan" hands is too stiff. He swats at the ball, rather than catches it.

Over the years, many major league shortstops have come from Latin America. Their childhood heroes were Aparicio and Concepcion. When still a teenager, Guillen was spotted by one of Aparicio's uncles, a scout in the country of Venezuela. The uncle invited Guillen to live with him, and for three years this future Rookie of the Year award-winner was taught all the skills of his position.

Little leaguers might be interested to know that Guillen still practices every day. In fact, one of his routines is to catch lots of grounders while wearing a glove no bigger than his hand. A small glove forces him to stay down on the ball and watch it right into his hands. Today, even though he is a veteran big leaguer, Guillen still goes out on the field every couple of weeks to practice diving! There is an old saying in baseball that you "play as you practice." Players who dive for balls during practice develop that reaction. When game time comes around, they do not have to think about diving—they just do it.

*One of the all-time great baseball players of any era—
Willie Mays, named Rookie of the Year in 1951.*

Outfielders

Twenty-five outfielders have been named Rookie of the Year. There are at least two reasons for this high number. One, there are three times as many players to choose from. Two, outfielders carry big bats. Players who swat homers and RBIs are vote-getters.

A list of all-time great rookie outfielders would be long. Willie Mays won the prize in 1951. A spellbinding center fielder, Mays won on the strength of a .274 batting average (BA), with 20 homers. He went on a hitting, running and fielding spree that lasted 21 years. He is on everyone's list of top ten players of the modern era. At the plate, Mays finished his career with 523 homers and a lifetime .302 batting average. In the field, he is second only to Ty Cobb in games played, and is the all-time lifetime leader in putouts, with 7,095.

Frank Robinson was

Rookie Trivia

Q: Name the National League Rookie of the Year who, in the same season, also led the AAA Pacific Coast League Phoenix Giants in home runs.
A: Willie McCovey.

Q: In his 1981 rookie year, Tim Raines set a freshman record for stolen bases with 71. Name the Rookie of the Year winner who, in 1985, broke Raines' record by stealing 110!
A: Vince Coleman.

Q: During the years 1979-81, three Dodger pitchers won Rookie of the Year—who were they?
A: Rick Sutcliffe, Steve Howe and Fernando Valenzuela.

An early '80s rookie winner: Ron Kittle.

the sixth outfielder to be Rookie of the Year, winning every vote in 1956. A graceful right fielder with a deadly arm, as a hitter Robinson "owned" the plate. He crowded in on it fearlessly, daring pitchers to hit him. But, beyond "Robbie's" lifetime Hall of Fame career, he was also baseball's first black manager. Outspoken and eloquent, Robinson eventually desegregated the big league "front office" as well.

    Mays and Robinson dominated the '50s and '60s, giving way to a new generation of rooks that were good, but not near their greatness. The Cubs' Billy Williams (1961), Yankee Tom Tresh (1962), Tony Oliva (1964) of the Twins, and Tommy Agee (1966) are but four rookie standouts who played in the shadow of Mays and Robinson.

Every year of the 1970s brought a new Rookie of the Year superstar. Al Bumbry (1973), who started out with the Orioles, and Bake McBride (1974), who debuted with the Cards, have both turned in near-.300 careers. In 1975, Red Sox fans had both Fred Lynn and Jim Rice appear on the scene! Lynn won Rookie of the Year with 23-1/2 votes, and Rice came in second by half a vote. In spite of this vote, however, Rice proved to be the more consistent player. After nearly 20 years in the game, Rice leads Lynn in batting average, home runs and runs batted in.

During the last ten years, these Rookie of the Year outfielders have made claims to early fame: Darryl Strawberry (1983), Ron Kittle (1983), Vince Coleman (1985), and Jose Canseco (1986).

In his rookie year, Kittle had a .254 batting average and 35 homers. But injuries have plagued him, and after nine years he is struggling with a lifetime batting average barely over .230.

Strawberry is one of baseball's most talked-about players, and his stats are respectable. But he is not yet a Hall of Famer. After almost nine seasons, Strawberry has settled into a .270 batting average. His home-run output has increased year by year, and in 1988 he led the league with 39. Strawberry recently was traded to the Dodgers, where there's a good chance that he will flourish in his new blue-and-white uniform.

Principally a singles hitter with a .260 batting average, Coleman is simply one of the finest base-stealers to ever scorch the basepaths. He has wings on his feet. What Coleman lacks as a hitter, he makes up for with his speed. Averaging 100 stolen bases per season, he has a chance of breaking all records. In fact, Coleman might steal 1,000—if Rickey Henderson doesn't do it first.

Jim Rice lost the rookie derby to Red Sox teammate Fred Lynn by one-half vote. But Rice went on to lead Lynn in batting average, homers, and RBIs.

If any rookie ever looked and played like someone who might dominate the game like Mays and Robinson, that person is Jose Canseco. He is a controversial ballplayer. But there is no question that he has what it takes. He is young, brash and cocky. Winning Rookie of the Year on the strength of a .240 batting average (with 33 homers and 117 RBIs), his statistics continue to improve season by season. In 1988 Canseco opened a new category in the record books. Leading the league with 42 homers, he also stole 40 bases, which made him the first member of the "40-40 Club."

Lou Aparicio of the Chicago White Sox was rookie of the year in 1956.

Out To Break The Records

Each new major league season brings with it a fresh crop of rookies. Early in spring training and throughout the regular season, all eyes are upon them. In many cases, rookies are expected to fill the shoes of veteran ballplayers whose time has come to retire. While watching these young men play, fans ask themselves, "Will he be the next Willie Mays?" Or the next Mike Schmidt, or Pete Rose, or Nolan Ryan?

Rookies are the hustling, up-and-coming competition every veteran worries about. Hungry, desperate for a chance to play and show what they can do, rookies give the game new energy. They are the future. Bigger, stronger, faster, and having had the advantages of better training and techniques, they give us a glimpse of what the game will be like ten or 20 years from now. Also, they are the players who most believe that "records are meant to be broken."

We have read how difficult it is to judge the long-term success of a ballplayer on the basis of a rookie year. Superstars are few and far between. Of the hundreds of rookies who appear every ten years, most will enjoy respectable careers, but only a few will go on to Hall of Fame greatness. As we read about those who have won the Rookie of the Year award, let's not forget how much of an honor it is just to get a chance to try out for a big

1972 AL Rookie of the Year Carlton Fisk was still going strong in 1990.

league team.

    A rookie playing in his first big league game is fulfilling the dreams of fans and little leaguers everywhere. Coming to the plate or trotting out on the field for the first time, the rookie is the symbol of potential. He is the product of months and years of practice and dedication. Barely 20 years old, he is out there playing with the aging veterans he idolized as a youngster. Now it's his turn to show his stuff.

Glossary

EARNED RUN AVERAGE (ERA). A statistic that rates pitchers. If you're a manager, you want a pitcher with a low earned run average.

GOLD GLOVE AWARD. The honor given at the end of each season to one player from every position in both leagues. Those who win are considered great defensive players.

HANDS. Good infielders are said to have good "hands." Sometimes they are said to have hands "soft as a bird dog's mouth." Bad infielders have hands made of iron, or "frying pan" hands.

HOT BOX. Third base, the position that receives a lot of "blue darters" and scorching ground balls.

MOST VALUABLE PLAYER (MVP). A player from each league who has had the best all-around season. Players in the All-Star Game, the league championship series, and the World Series, also receive MVP awards.

ROOKIE. A first-year player. A player is a rookie if he has not accumulated more than 130 at-bats, 45 innings pitched or 45 days on a major league roster before September 1st of a given season. The term probably comes from the military word "recruit."

ROOKIE OF THE YEAR. At the end of every season, one rookie from each league earns the award for best overall performance.

Bibliography

Books

Durant, John. *The Story of Baseball in Words and Pictures.* New York: Hastings House, 1973.

Falkner, David. *Nine Sides of the Diamond.* New York: Times Books/Random House, 1990.

Kaplan, Jim. *Playing the Field.* Chapel Hill: Algonquin Books of Chapel Hill, 1987.

Ritter, Lawrence, and Donald Honig. *The 100 Greatest Baseball Players of All Time.* New York: Crown Publishers, 1986.

Thorn, John, and Pete Palmer. *Total Baseball.* New York: Warner Books, 1989.

Periodicals

Wulf, Steve. "The Big Sweep." *Sports Illustrated*, October 29, 1990: 18.

About The Author

Doug Marx is a 41-year-old poet and freelance writer who, when not reading books or writing them, suffers from "baseball on the brain." Having played at the little league, high school and college levels, he now plays a hot third base for the Grass Stains, a men's softball team. Marx, who spent the better part of his childhood bouncing rubber-coated hardballs off brick walls, has also spent many years coaching boys' and girls' little league teams. He lives in Portland, Oregon, with his wife and three children.

Index

Agee, Tommy, 38
Allen Dick, 29, 30
Aparicio, Luis, 33, 35

Bench, Johnny, 15, 17
Bumbry, Al, 39

Canseco, Jose, 39-41
Carew, Rod, 25-27
Castino, John, 29
Cepeda, Orlando, 7, 19
Coleman, Vince, 7, 17, 37, 39-40

Dark, Alvin, 33
Davis, Al, 19

Fisk, Carlton, 7, 15, 17

Gilliam, Junior, 23-25, 27
Gooden, Dwight, 5, 13, 23
Guillen, Ozzie, 33, 34-35

Hansen, Ron, 33
Hargrove, Mike, 19
Horner, Bob, 29, 30-31
Howe, Steve, 12, 37

Kittle, Ron, 39
Kubek, Tony, 33
Kuenn, Harvey, 33

Lynn, Fred, 23, 39

Mays, Willie, 5, 37, 38, 43
McBride, Bake, 39
McCovey, Willie, 7, 17, 37

McGwire, Mark, 9, 19, 20-21
Munson, Thurman, 15-17
Murray, Eddie, 19, 20

Newcombe, Don, 11

Oliva, Tony, 38

Rice, Jim, 39
Righetti, Dave, 13
Ripken, Jr., Cal, 29, 33, 34
Robinson, Frank, 7, 38-39
Robinson, Jackie, 5, 7, 11, 23, 27
rookie(s)
    defined, 7
    origin of word, 6-7
    Rookie of the Year Award, 7-9
Rose, Pete, 5, 25, 43

Sabo, Chris, 29, 31
Santiago, Benito, 7-9, 15, 17
Sax, Steve, 27
Seaver, Tom, 11-12, 23
Strawberry, Darryl, 39
Sutcliffe, Rick, 13, 37

Tresh, Tom, 38

Valenzuela, Fernando, 12-13, 23, 37

Weiss, Walt, 33-34
Williams, Billy, 38
Williams, Earl, 15
Worrell, Todd, 13

Picture Credits

ALLSPORT USA: 4, 8, 34, 40 (Otto Greule, Jr.); 14, 16 (Stephen Dunn);
    18 (John Cordes); 22 (B. Schwartzman); 26 (Rick Stewart); 28 (Scott
    Halleran); 32 (J. Rettaliata); 38 (Jonathan Daniel); 11, 30 (ALLSPORT)
National Baseball Library, Cooperstown, NY: 6, 10, 12, 20, 21, 24, 36, 44
UPI: 42

ALBANY LIBRARY
UTICA CITY SCHOOLS

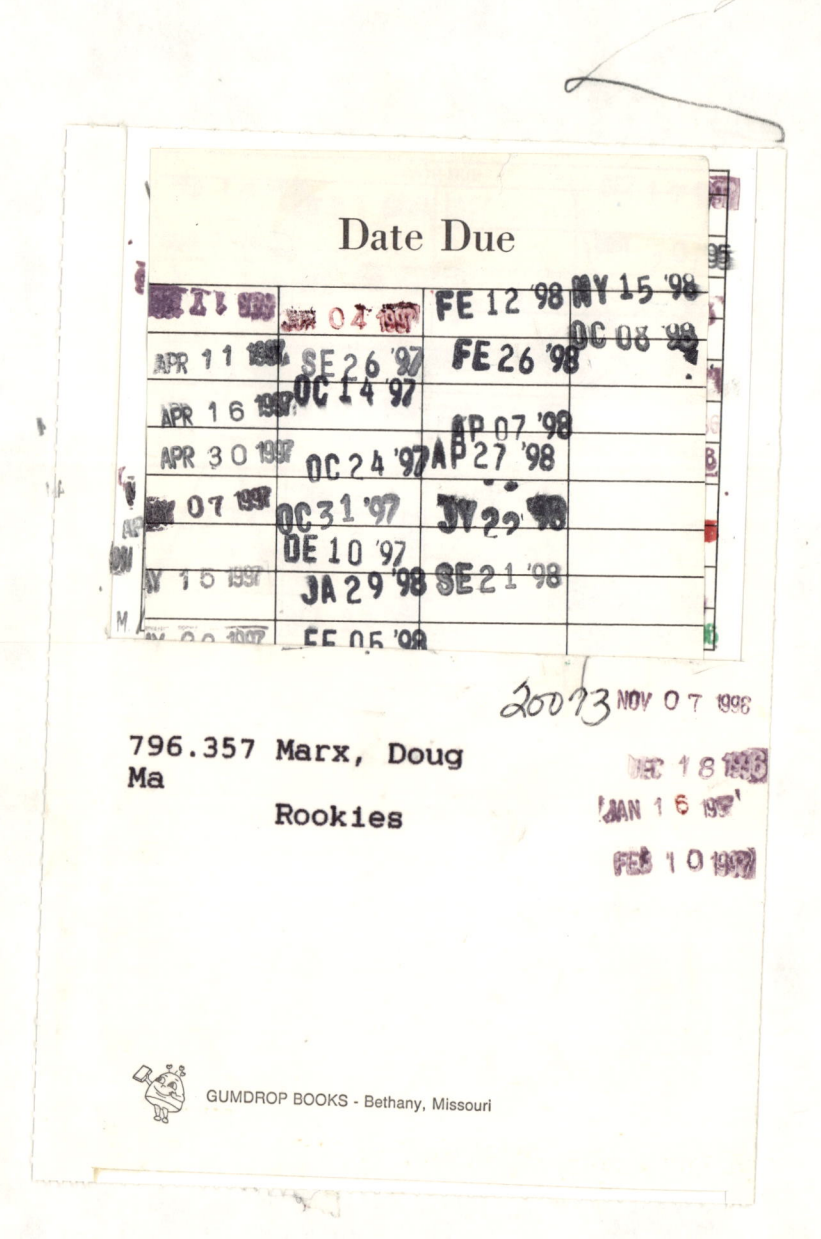

Date Due

	JN 04 '97	FE 12 '98	MY 15 '98
APR 11	SE 26 '97	FE 26 '98	OC 08 '98
APR 16	OC 14 '97		
APR 30	OC 24 '97	AP 07 '98	
MY 07	OC 31 '97	AP 27 '98	
	DE 10 '97	JY 22 '98	
NV 15	JA 29 '98	SE 21 '98	
	FE 05 '98		

20073 NOV 07 1996

796.357 Marx, Doug
Ma
      Rookies

DEC 18 1996
JAN 16 1997
FEB 10 1997

GUMDROP BOOKS - Bethany, Missouri